To Stand Forever

Greg Gosdin
Illustrated by Tom McNeely

A Harcourt Achieve Imprint

www.Rigby.com
1-800-531-5015

Literacy by Design Leveled Readers: *To Stand Forever*

ISBN-13: 978-1-4189-3923-6
ISBN-10:   1-4189-3923-4

Printed in China
1 2 3 4 5 6 7 8 985 13 12 11 10 09 08 07 06

Contents

∽ Chapter 1 ∽
Divided Loyalties

Enrique Esparza was having a great time. He and his best friends, Josué and Martin, were playing with long branches pulled from the tree in the neighbor's yard. These branches made terrific swords. They clacked loudly when knocked together. Enrique had shaved the bark from the end of his sword so he could get a firmer grip. Now he was battling Martin, blocking his friend's every move and thrusting forward when he had the chance.

The three friends chased each other up and down the dirt lane in front of Enrique's house, swords waving in the air. Their homemade shirts and pants protected them, mostly, from the coolness of the March afternoon, but out in the sun, the boys felt warm. Enrique ran barefoot since, like most children, he only wore shoes when he went to school or to church, or when it was too cold for bare feet.

But today was especially perfect for bare feet. Today was especially perfect for everything.

The year was 1836, and the town of San Antonio in the state of *Coahuila y Tejas*, Mexico, where ten-year-old Enrique and his family lived, had been a peaceful place for the last couple of months—ever since the fighting that had taken place that December had ended.

As dangerous and bloody as they'd been, the battles had happened for very important reasons. Enrique enjoyed listening to his father, Gregorio Esparza, speak about how he wanted his state to be a free country. Enrique always did his best to ask his father questions so he could understand what was happening around him.

The president of Mexico was a man named Santa Anna who had made himself dictator over his people as he came into power. This meant that he was the complete ruler of his country. He ordered his soldiers to arrest or kill anyone who did not obey him.

Gregorio Esparza believed that all people deserved to live in peace and freedom, and so, he wanted the state of Tejas to be its own country, free of the dictator Santa Anna. Gregorio had always taught Enrique that bullying was wrong. And now he felt that Mexico's government had become like a bully, forcing people to do whatever it wanted them to do.

Ana Esparza, Enrique's mother, believed that everyone deserved to be treated with dignity. She had often taken Enrique and his younger siblings to care for their neighbors when they were sick. Ana had also taken food to the *viejos*, or older people in the community, when there was extra food to spare. Enrique learned from her example. He loved to visit Señor Musquiz, the old man who lived down the street, especially because Señor Musquiz always had interesting stories to tell.

Enrique had heard his parents discussing places like Zacatecas and the nearby town of Gonzales. They said that Santa Anna had ordered his soldiers to march to Zacatecas, where they took people's homes, land, and guns. When the people resisted, they were all killed.

After that the soldiers continued on to Gonzales. There the people refused to give up their cannon to Santa Anna's troops. It was the only one they had–they needed it for protection. They fought to keep it, and after a short battle, the people of Gonzales drove Santa Anna's troops away. Luckily, no one had been killed in the battle.

Over the winter Santa Anna's soldiers had taken over an old Spanish church mission in San Antonio called the Alamo. They used it for their home base and wouldn't let the people of San Antonio use it any more.

This was too much for Gregorio to stand. He worried that what had happened in Zacatecas and Gonzales could also happen in San Antonio. He joined a company of volunteers, and they drove Santa Anna's soldiers out of the Alamo.

During the battle the air was filled with the loud booms of cannons and gunfire, and until Gregorio finally made it home safely several days later, Enrique worried that his father had been hurt . . . or worse.

It seemed to Enrique that this battle had caused many arguments among the adults. Some, like his and Josué's parents, were opposed to Santa Anna. But some, like Martin's parents, felt loyal to the Mexican government. They felt that it was the Americans living in Tejas, and not Santa Anna, who were to blame for the fighting.

Enrique's uncle Francisco also believed that supporting Santa Anna's government was the right thing to do. Francisco joined Santa Anna's army and fought against Gregorio that past December in San Antonio. Gregorio had been forced to fight against his own brother, and Enrique could tell how much this hurt his father. Even though they had won the battle, and Santa Anna's soldiers had been driven out of the Alamo, Gregorio seemed much quieter than usual when he got home.

There were rumors that Santa Anna and his soldiers were coming back, but those rumors had been around for a while. Now people mostly seemed to ignore them. Enrique himself had once been afraid of soldiers suddenly attacking, but the weeks and months had passed and still nothing had happened. And so he had stopped worrying about it too much.

Besides, it was early March. If any soldiers were coming, they would wait until later in the spring when it was much easier for them to travel—or so most people said.

Enrique knocked his wooden sword against Martin's. "I'm winning," he said.

"No, you're not!" Martin shot back, blocking Enrique's sword before it could touch his shoulder. "I am. I've gotten you three times!"

"Is it my turn yet?" Josué asked.

Just then, Enrique heard his mother's voice calling him from down the block. "Enrique? Enrique, come here. Quickly! Tell your friends that they must run home right away."

Enrique stopped the game, but not before Martin touched him on the leg with his sword. He noticed for the first time how strangely empty the streets were. A few people were rushing home, looking very worried. Enrique saw a man shutting his windows tight.

"What's happening?" asked Josué.

"I don't know," replied Enrique.

"Listen," said Martin.

The bell in the San Fernando church tower began to ring. There were men up there shouting down to people on the ground. The church was several blocks away, so Enrique couldn't quite understand what the crowd was saying, but by

their harsh words, he knew that something bad was happening.

Then he saw a few people pointing at something in the distance.

"Come on!" Enrique said to the other boys.

They ran all the way to the San Fernando church, where they could see what the men had been shouting about.

Coming over the Alazan Hills were soldiers on horses, thousands of them, pouring down toward San Antonio. Enrique thought they moved like a herd of ants covering the ground.

"It's Santa Anna's army," Enrique said.

The soldiers wore brightly colored uniforms, and some were in armor, which shone in the afternoon sun. Many had what looked like spears with fierce metal points. They carried these weapons upright like flagpoles.

Others had muskets and swords hanging from the sides of their horses. The soldiers at the front carried flags, which whipped angrily in the wind.

Like a river of men and horses, Santa Anna's army flowed slowly over the hills, coming closer and closer. And now in the distance, Enrique could see men on foot. These soldiers marched side by side in long lines, with horse-drawn wagons among them.

Enrique, Martin, and Josué ran to the open square in front of the Alamo. Many people were rushing inside the old mission, taking wagons, horses, and a few cattle with them. Others were carrying bundles of clothing, blankets, pots and pans, guns, and gun powder—everything they could hold. Other families were hitching teams of oxen to wagons so they could head out of town.

The boys turned and saw Santa Anna's soldiers ride into the square, their horses kicking up huge clouds of dust under their thunderous hooves. A man dressed in finer clothes than the rest of the soldiers rode into the center of the town square. Silver armor hung from his horse. The reins were also decorated with silver, and metallic ornaments were woven into the horse's mane and tail, making it look like a metal monster.

The man wore black pants, shiny black boots, and a tall hat with long feathers flowing downward and waving in the wind. The medals on his chest and the gold tassels on his shoulders sparkled in the sun.

The man reined in his horse and sat in his saddle without saying a word. He gazed down at the soldiers flooding the square and the frightened people scurrying about. Then he dismounted, handed the reins to one of his soldiers, and began walking across the square in the direction of a house in the northwest corner of the plaza.

The soldier holding the reins bowed his head and said, "Your Excellency."

Enrique heard amazement in Martin's voice as he softly said, "That's Santa Anna."

Chapter 2
Santa Anna in San Antonio

Enrique was suddenly terrified. His mouth had gone dry, and his knees were shaking. He looked at Martin, who did not seem frightened at all.

"That's him!" Martin said excitedly, tugging on Enrique's arm. "That's Santa Anna! My father said that our president will get rid of all the troublemakers, and that anybody who stands with the Americans is a traitor!"

Enrique was stung by his friend's words. Martin's father knew that Gregorio had helped drive Santa Anna's soldiers from San Antonio.

"My father isn't a troublemaker," said Enrique, "or a traitor. Santa Anna is a bully!" Enrique looked his friend in the eye, not wanting to argue, but not wanting Martin to speak badly of his father, either.

"I'm sorry," Martin said quietly. "I didn't mean it that way."

Enrique was about to say something to hurt Martin's feelings, just as his had been hurt. But then he remembered his mother's words: *Everybody has an opinion, Enrique. Just be sure of what you believe, then do what you know is right.*

"It's OK, Martin," Enrique replied.

The boys ran home to tell their families what was happening down at the Alamo. They arrived at Enrique's house first, and as Martin and Josué ran on to their own houses, Enrique suddenly felt like there was a great distance between him and his friends. In a strange way, he was afraid he might never see them again.

When Enrique went inside, he saw that his father had a visitor.

Colorado Smith and Gregorio sat at the kitchen table, drinking coffee and speaking in heated voices about Santa Anna's army. Colorado Smith was from America. He'd come to Tejas to settle, and he was also in favor of freeing San Antonio from the dictator Santa Anna.

Enrique's baby sister slept in her crib near the table, and his two younger brothers huddled by the fireplace. Ana gave Enrique a stern look for running off when he should have come in out of danger, but then she gave him a big hug, thankful that all her children were home safely.

"We have no choice," Mr. Smith said.

"Santa Anna's army has taken over the town," Gregorio said, "but we can take shelter in the Alamo and wait for help."

Ana looked at her husband the way she often did, as though she could read Gregorio's thoughts. Enrique's heart was pounding, and he felt a little sick to his stomach. Things were beginning to feel out of control, like he was riding in a wagon with a broken brake lever.

Ana turned away from Mr. Smith and said, "Come, children, let's get packed. We'll be taking shelter in the Alamo."

After Mr. Smith had left, everyone rushed around the house, collecting pots, pans, blankets for the baby, corn meal, and lard for cooking–anything they could carry. Gregorio took his long musket from above the fireplace, then he slung a powder horn and several bags of musket balls over his shoulder.

Enrique caught his father's eye as he grabbed his leather coat and hat. His father gave him a reassuring smile, then motioned with his head that they should go.

Like a small parade, the family left the only home Enrique had ever known. He was born in

San Antonio, and its low adobe buildings were his world. He knew and loved its fences, its dust, its chicken coops, its stables, and its blacksmith shops. San Antonio was where his family and friends lived—was it all about to be taken away?

A cart, piled high with blankets, cooking equipment, and Josué's family, rolled past, pulled by two oxen.

"Hey, Josué, where are you going?" Enrique called, remembering that Josué's family also disliked Santa Anna.

"We're going to my uncle's farm," Josué replied as the cart rolled away. "My father says we'll be safe there. He says it's too dangerous to stay in San Antonio—even in the Alamo!"

A few moments later, Josué and his family were gone. Enrique, arms full of blankets for his baby sister, looked up at his parents. He hoped Josué's father was wrong, and that the Alamo would be safe.

Enrique's family, loaded down with their belongings, quickly approached the Alamo. As they drew closer, they passed over a short bridge running over a small stream. One branch of this stream flowed under the Alamo's walls, carrying water to the people inside. Normally, there was plenty of water in the stream, but Enrique saw only mud. Worse, in the distance he saw Santa Anna's soldiers shoveling dirt into the stream, purposely cutting off the water supply to the old Spanish mission.

Enrique became very afraid again—the sun was setting fast and soldiers were everywhere. They were digging ditches and holes and setting up rows and rows of cannons. There were more cannons than Enrique could count, all aimed at the Alamo.

And we're going into the Alamo, Enrique thought, feeling sick to his stomach again.

The Esparza family approached the main gates that led inside the Alamo. The mission had a tall fortress wall that surrounded a group of small buildings. It was in those smaller buildings inside the fortress wall that they would find shelter.

To his right was an old building made of adobe; to his left, a wall of dirt. Several men stood around, their guns at their sides. Men also stood atop the wall. In the darkness they looked like fence posts.

"Come on!" said Gregorio loudly. He led his family around to the back of the Alamo. There was a small window cut into the tall fortress wall. Gregorio looked into the window and called in English, "Hey in there, it's Gregorio!"

A man suddenly appeared, replying in English, "Come on up, but hurry!"

It was almost dark, and as the sun began to set, Gregorio lifted Enrique's mother up to the man, who pulled her inside. Next went his baby sister, then his brothers, and lastly Gregorio handed Enrique up to the man.

As Enrique jumped down to the dirt floor on the other side, he saw that he had crawled over a huge cannon. It wasn't a window he'd just crawled through–it was a cannon hole!

After his eyes had gotten used to the
darkness in the room, Enrique saw that he
was standing inside the chapel of the ancient
mission's church. He was on top of a hill of dirt
piled high so that the cannon could be aimed
out of the hole. Shadows flickered and dark
shapes danced silently in this scary place.

Gregorio crawled through the window and
landed softly on the ground. Then, the man who
had helped them said, "Come on. I'll show you
where your family can stay."

They were led through the large double doors of the chapel, through a small courtyard, and into a little room. Making a sweeping motion with his hand, the man said, "Here it is. It's not much, but it's the safest part of the Alamo."

"Thank you," said Enrique's father. "We'll get settled, then I'll join you."

"It's good to have you with us, Gregorio," replied the man.

Inside the dark, windowless little adobe room, the floor was nothing but dirt ground. There was a place in one wall that was blackened from years of small cooking fires. Gregorio held a lantern the man had given him, and its light helped the family put their belongings away.

Out beyond the walls of the Alamo, the world was full of soldiers, horses, cannons, and guns. Uncle Francisco was also out there, in Santa Anna's army. He was among those that his parents said were the enemy. Inside the Alamo walls, Enrique was with his family, but everything was strange and frightening.

Was fighting Santa Anna the right thing to do? It seemed difficult to understand. If, like his parents said, the right thing to do was something he would know in his heart, then why couldn't everyone know it? If right is clearly right, and wrong is clearly wrong, then why were all these people ready to fight each other?

A blanket spread out beneath them, Enrique laid down with his brothers on the dirt floor of the little room, yet he didn't think he would get much sleep that night.

⪎ Chapter 3 ⪏
The Fighting Begins

"Open the gate!"

Enrique woke to the sound of someone shouting. It was morning, and he was lying on the blanket his mother had placed on the dirt floor. He had indeed slept, exhausted from fear and confusion.

He scrambled to his feet and, peering out the door across the courtyard, saw his father standing with a group of men at the main gate. The gate was open, and just inside were two of Santa Anna's soldiers, mounted on splendidly decorated horses.

One soldier held a tall pole with a white flag at the top, and the other reached down and handed a piece of paper to a man Enrique did not recognize. Gregorio told him later that the man was William Travis, commander of the Alamo.

Travis read the paper, then looked up at the soldiers and across at the group of men on the ground. He said something to the soldiers, who turned their horses around and galloped away through the gate. Once they were out of sight, the gate was slammed shut.

Further along the wall to the right of the gate was another dirt hill leading up to the top of the fort wall. An enormous cannon loomed at the top, pointing out toward the enemy. It was surrounded by several men, facing outward into the morning sky.

The cold March wind whipped through the plaza. No one said anything, and it seemed to Enrique that they were all waiting for the man with the paper in his hand to make a declaration.

A moment later the man shouted, "Fire!"

BOOM! The huge cannon at the top of the dirt hill erupted with smoke and a roar!

The men scattered in all directions, shouting orders. Enrique ran out into the plaza toward his father, wanting desperately to know what was happening.

"Enrique, come back!" his mother yelled from the doorway of the little room. "Now!" Standing there in her long dress and shawl and waving her arms, she looked like a mother bird. As he ran to her, Enrique felt he would be safe.

Enrique believed his mother was very brave. In fact, he realized that he had never seen his mother afraid. "We're going to stay inside for a while," she said matter-of-factly as she pulled Enrique inside their shelter. She shut the door against the sound of people running and shouting. "Enrique, please get the corn meal. We need to make the *masa*."

As the children began the tasks their mother had assigned them, Enrique tried not to think about where they were.

Suddenly, he heard a more distant boom, like thunder from an afternoon storm. A couple of seconds later, there was a loud hissing sound, like when a blacksmith lowers a hot horseshoe into water.

As the hissing sound drew closer, Enrique's mother stopped and looked up at the low ceiling–now she looked afraid.

SLAM! The wall next to Enrique shuddered with a deafening blast. He felt like someone had kicked him in the chest, and he had trouble breathing.

Dust flew everywhere, and Enrique and his brothers ran to their mother, who held them and their baby sister all as tightly as she could. She covered her baby's face with her shawl.

Enrique had never heard anything so loud in all his life, and although his ears were ringing, he could still hear the younger children crying, and his mother shushing them.

Enrique had never been so afraid. He wondered if his father would be coming for them soon, or if he was even all right.

☙ Chapter 4 ❧
The Shadow in the Doorway

"Fire!" yelled a man from across the courtyard. His voice was carried through the open doorway by a stale wind.

BOOM! A cannon fired.

BOOM! Another.

BOOM! And another.

The world seemed to be tearing itself apart.

The ringing in Enrique's ears continued as the cannons thundered and the rifles and muskets popped and spat. The smell of gunpowder was so thick that he could taste it as it floated on the air. The sounds of people yelling also came into the room, and occasionally, Enrique could hear the cry of a child.

There are other children here, too, he thought.

Another cannon ball slammed into the wall near the room, scattering pieces of adobe across the ground. Enrique's hair was white with adobe dust. He was so afraid that he thought he might cry, but he couldn't even do that. All he could do was cling to his mother.

BOOM! The ground shook beneath the terrified family as the sound of battle raged all around. It was as though hundreds of angry giants were trying to crush the whole world.

Enrique had no idea how long it lasted, but at that moment, the noise unexpectedly stopped. Was the battle over? All Enrique could hear was the ringing in his ears and the sound of his heart pounding wildly. But gradually the ringing seemed to go away, the dust and smoke in the air began to clear a little, and Enrique could hear scattered voices here and there out in the courtyard.

A shadow filled the doorway.

The large figure of a man stood there. The sunlight shone behind him so that he was nothing more than a dark shape against the bright midday sun. As Enrique's eyes adjusted, he began to recognize the man. It was his father!

He ran to him, jumping into his arms, laughing and crying at the same time. His father smelled like gunpowder and dirt.

"Whoa, Enrique," Gregorio laughed. "I'm glad to see you, too! Is everyone OK?"

"Yes, we're OK," said Ana, brushing the adobe dust out of her hair. "We're just a little shaken up."

Gregorio rushed inside the little room, wrapped his arms around his wife, and they both held each other for a long time, their children between them.

≈ Chapter 5 ≈
Standing Up to Bullies

"Sure, Mama," replied Enrique when, the next afternoon, his mother asked him to go and get some water. Santa Anna's soldiers had cut off the water flowing into the Alamo, but the people inside had dug a well within the fort.

Enrique grabbed the old leather bucket just inside the doorway and headed out across the courtyard. The gunfire had stopped for a while this afternoon, and everyone was taking advantage of the time to gather wood, fetch water, and shake the dirt out of blankets. Several cooking fires burned around the mission, making the air smell like smoke and meat. Over in the pen, the cows mooed and the goats bleated. Enrique had taken his turn milking the cows that morning. He'd delivered the milk to the other families before sunrise, just before the fighting had begun for the day.

Across the open courtyard, he saw William Travis talking with a few men. Travis was the man who had taken the message from Santa Anna's soldiers that first morning. Travis had also ordered that the cannon be fired to show that the Alamo refused to surrender. Another man, Jim Bowie, had also been in command, but he had fallen sick with a terrible illness and was resting in one of the rooms deep inside the Alamo's walls.

Enrique lowered his bucket into the well, filled it, then struggled to raise it back up. He'd barely set the bucket on the ground when he heard the scream. Looking across the courtyard, he saw a girl, much younger than himself, wailing and pointing at three boys who were throwing small rocks at a cat. The boys had the cat cornered, and it hissed as each rock hit the wall behind it. The boys laughed and pointed, calling the cat "Santa Anna."

"Hey, stop it!" Enrique yelled at the boys, but they ignored him.

He became angry—the boys were bullying both the cat and the little girl—so he gathered his courage and walked right past the boys to the cat.

"Get out of the way!" shouted one of the boys. "We'll hit you if you don't."

WHAP. A rock hit Enrique in the back, but he ignored it.

When he reached the cat, it hissed and bared its fangs. Enrique knew he would have to be quick. Taking a deep breath, he grabbed the cat with lightning speed. He held it by the scruff of the neck, the same way a mother cat holds its kittens in her mouth. Enrique knew this wouldn't hurt the cat; instead, it would make it relax.

The boys were quiet now as Enrique walked past, still ignoring them, and handed the cat to the wide-eyed little girl, who hugged it tightly.

"What's your name?" Enrique asked.

"Emily," she said with a grateful smile. Then she ran off, holding the cat close to her.

Enrique turned and looked at the boys, his heart beating fast. No one said anything. He picked up his bucket of water and went back to his family's room.

⤳ Chapter 6 ⤺
An Overheard Conversation

BOOM! A cannon fired, the latest in a long line of many shots ringing out over the last several days. Nothing seemed to change. One day was just like another. Unable to see anything outside the walls, Enrique wondered if anyone was winning this battle.

Then the cannon fell silent, and Enrique was amazed at how loud the silence was around him. Without the thunder of battle, the occasional shout from someone on the wall seemed like the fragile sound of a bird carried on the breeze.

Enrique felt so tired. The way his body ached reminded him of the afternoon he and Josué had dragged a huge log up from the river. They had wanted something on which to stand tall as they played. He wondered now if Josué was OK.

Without the horrible sound of gunfire, it seemed that the whole fort was letting itself breathe. Some of the men began to leave their posts, coming down from the walls or straying from the fences. Some of the families began to emerge from their rooms, like rabbits from holes.

Then came a shout: "Riders approaching under a white flag!" The last time Enrique had heard those words, the fighting had begun.

Everyone around the gate seemed to get tense again as someone ordered, "Open the gate!" Once opened, several of Santa Anna's soldiers entered, just as before. The lead soldier again carried a tall pole with a white flag on top. They were all in splendid uniform, while everyone inside the fort looked filthy and exhausted.

Travis and several men approached the soldiers, and everyone watched each other very closely as a soldier handed Travis a piece of paper–just like on the first day of fighting.

Travis read the message, looked at his men, looked back at Santa Anna's soldiers, and said something Enrique couldn't hear. The soldiers turned and rode away as the Alamo's men closed the gate behind them–just like before.

But unlike before, Travis and his men walked silently back into the commander's quarters. There was no gunfire, no shouting.

"Enrique, let's go back inside and wait for your father," said Ana nervously.

Enrique and his brothers sat on the floor, eating tortillas and drinking cups of broth, while his little sister slept on her blanket next to them. Ana built a fire each night outside the doorway. She put her cast-iron cooking pot over the fire to cook their dinner. Tonight she had used a beef bone to make broth, and to Enrique, it was a feast.

When his father arrived, he sat among them, smiling wearily.

"What did the soldiers want?" Ana asked.

Gregorio cast a glance over at his children, then he replied gently, "Let's discuss this outside."

They both got up and stepped outside. Enrique hid inside the doorway so he could hear, just like the time at home when he'd learned that his father was going to fight Santa Anna's soldiers. Enrique knew he would never forget that night.

Enrique remembered how his father had come home, deep in thought. As he hung his hat on the peg just inside the door, his mother moved close to him, thinking she was out of earshot of the children.

"What is it, Gregorio?"

"Gonzales," he said. "Troops have moved in with orders to take their cannon."

"That would leave them without anything to protect themselves with," Ana whispered.

"Exactly. They'd be easier for Santa Anna to control." Gregorio was silent for a moment before declaring, "I'm going to volunteer."

"For what?"

"Juan Seguin is putting together a group of fighters, and I'm joining."

"To do what?" Ana asked, although in her heart she already knew the answer.

"To stand up for our rights."

"You know what will be said, Gregorio. They'll say that you stood with the Americans against your own country," she said.

"Maybe," he replied, "but most people just want to live in peace and quiet here in northern Mexico. Our government invited settlers here, promising land and freedom, but now it puts chains on us. All we want is what the government promised us, yet it tries to fight us for it."

"But we have freedom as Mexicans," Ana protested. "We can go where we want and do what we want."

"No, we can only do what Santa Anna allows. The whole country is like his prison, and we're his prisoners. He leaves us alone when we pay his taxes and let his soldiers take what they want from us. But if he wants more, we must give more, or he will kill us. Remember Zacatecas? When the people stood up for themselves, he killed them all."

Enrique's parents were silent for a time.

"Even if we are free prisoners, we are still prisoners," Gregorio whispered. "And when he no longer needs us, what then?"

There was silence between them for a little longer, while the fire in the fireplace quietly popped. It warmed their home, filling it with a golden glow.

Then Enrique's mother slowly nodded her head, her face set firm. "Very well. We will stand up to Santa Anna."

That night seemed so long ago now, as the battle of the Alamo raged all around Enrique and his family.

"What did the note say?" Ana asked her husband. "What did Travis say to you?"

"Santa Anna is getting ready to take the fort," Gregorio replied, "but he's giving us a chance to get our families out of here. He says women and children will be allowed to leave safely."

"Do you believe he'll keep his word?" Ana asked fearfully.

"No, and I do not want to risk you and the children," said Gregorio. "However, Santa Anna also said that any Mexicans that fought with the Americans would be considered traitors, so if you stay here . . . " He couldn't finish his sentence.

The air hung crisp and cool with a slight breeze that smelled like smoke, and Enrique's mother was silent for a moment before asking, "What was Travis's answer?"

"He said we'll agree to it," replied Gregorio. "The women and children are to leave the Alamo."

"Then he's planning on staying and fighting no matter what?" Ana's voice was choked with tears. "And you're going to stay with him?"

"We're expecting help from James Fannin in Goliad. He's coming with several hundred men. Travis thinks that with their help we'll be able to drive the soldiers out of San Antonio once and for all!"

There was another long moment of silence before Ana spoke again. "But what do *you* think, Gregorio?" she asked.

"No one has come to help us since the Gonzales volunteers arrived," he replied thoughtfully. "With the men we have, there's no way we can win. But if we surrender, who knows what Santa Anna will do to us? And who knows what will happen to you and the children? At the very least, we'll lose our homes, but we could lose everything–even our lives."

"And if we fight and lose, things will turn out the same."

"What do you mean 'we'?" Gregorio asked.

"We've always stayed together as a family, and we're not going to change that now. If you stay, then the children and I will stay," said Ana.

"Very well," Gregorio said, and Enrique felt his body go cold with fear.

Gregorio and Ana almost tripped over Enrique as they re-entered the room. They stared at him, startled, but there was no need to say anything—they knew he had heard everything. Enrique's parents opened their arms, gathering their son to them, and the family held each other tightly.

⤳ Chapter 7 ⤳
No Help from Fannin

The sun was high in the sky, and the golden sunshine made the day warmer, even though a chilled March wind could still be cold when it rushed past. Things had been quiet for over a day now, so Enrique crept out into the courtyard. He was surprised to see Emily standing in the doorway of her family's room, cradling her cat. Emily's family also must have felt that it was just as dangerous for them to leave as it was to stay.

Enrique could sometimes hear a cow mooing over in the pen, or a goat bleating. All around him the adobe walls rose up, blocking his view of anything beyond. The walls now had craters and holes blown into them, and chunks of adobe were strewn about the courtyard, blasted out of the walls by incoming cannon balls.

Enrique had an idea.

He went to the chapel, then ran up the dirt ramp to the cannon pointing out the hole to the east where his family had come in that first night. Three men rested near the cannon, and when they saw him, they smiled. Enrique scrambled up the large wooden wheel of the cannon, trying to climb on top of it so that he could see out the hole. One of the men rose and helped him up. When Enrique peered out, his mouth went dry with fear.

There were soldiers as far as he could see in every direction. Some stood in straight lines, some walked around tents and campfires, and some tended horses. There were so many of them Enrique thought there might not be a number high enough to count them all. And he saw cannons, lots and lots of cannons lined up in rows, all aimed at him.

He lost his grip and landed in the dirt. The men said nothing as they helped him to his feet, but one of them nodded as if to say, *I know, son. It's pretty scary out there.*

Suddenly a voice out in the courtyard shouted, "Rider approaching! Looks like Bonham!" This got the attention of the men attending the cannon, and Enrique ran with them down the dirt hill and out into the chilled spring air.

"Stay back, son," said one of the men, and Enrique slowed as the men joined several others out in the courtyard, surrounding the rider who had just entered the Alamo. As the gates rapidly closed behind the rider, he dismounted, and Enrique lost sight of him in the group of men. A moment later Enrique's father walked out of the group, coming over slowly and looking very tired and serious.

He walked up to Enrique, took his hand, and the two of them went back to the little room that had become their home. Ana was feeding Enrique's baby sister, and as her eyes met Gregorio's, Enrique knew the news from the rider had not been good.

"Fannin is not coming," said his father. "No one is coming to help us."

This hit Enrique like one of the cannon balls. His father had not even waited to talk with his mother privately. He'd said it in front of the whole family since the news affected them all.

"Now it's just us," Gregorio added. "Travis is going to speak to us all later tonight."

Ana nodded, rocking Enrique's sister who had fallen asleep in her arms.

Chapter 8
Crossing the Line

Though the breeze that night was as gentle as a whisper, it seemed colder than usual. Enrique, unable to sleep, peered out of the doorway of the small room. His younger brothers were asleep on their blankets, and his mother was dozing with his baby sister cradled firmly in her arms.

Enrique was exhausted from the fear caused by days and days of gunfire and people yelling. He was very hungry, having eaten only broth and tortillas for days. His body ached, and he couldn't remember the last time he'd had a bath.

Earlier that evening his father had kissed his mother on the forehead just before going out. He went to meet the men in the courtyard, as Colonel Travis had ordered. There was no fighting that night—in fact, all of San Antonio seemed to have fallen silent.

The men outside were standing side by side, listening to Travis's every word. Even Mr. Bowie was out there with the rest of the men. He lay on his cot because his illness had gotten much worse.

The men's faces were lit by a single fire that

burned outside a doorway, casting dark shadows around the courtyard. Enrique tried to listen, but they were too far away for him to hear what was being said.

Suddenly, Travis drew his sword, walked to one end of the line of men, and dragged the blade of the sword along the ground, making a line in the dirt in front of them all. Travis was on one side, and all the others, including Enrique's father, were on the other side.

"I now want every man who is determined to stay here and die with me to come across this line," Travis said.

Enrique saw each of the men, all except one, step over the line, joining Travis. A few of the men even carried Mr. Bowie on his cot. Enrique's father stepped over the line, too. No one was smiling, since this was a very serious thing that they'd done.

Enrique felt his stomach tighten into a knot. He had never felt so alone, so cut off from his friends and the life he'd once known.

The one man who had not stepped over the line ran away into the shadows. Part of Enrique felt like running, too, but these days his family was all that he had, and he couldn't bear the thought of losing them.

A few minutes later, Gregorio came back to their room, knelt down, and hugged Enrique. "I need to talk to your mother. I don't want you to worry, OK? We'll be back in a little while."

Enrique's eyes followed his mother and father until they were out of sight around a corner. Then, looking in the direction of Travis's line in the dirt, he darted out of the room and across the courtyard.

There it was, nothing more than a small scratch in the dust stretching out in front of him, dividing the now empty courtyard area.

Slowly, Enrique lifted one foot, touching his toe to the dirt on the other side of the line, as if checking the temperature of water in a stream. He took a deep breath, and stepped over the line.

Did he feel any different? He wasn't sure, but he thought he did.

Enrique ran back to the little room and was soon fast asleep. He never heard his parents come in.

∾ Chapter 9 ∾
The Last Defense

A cannon roared–BOOM!

Guns fired–Pop! Pop! Pop!

Enrique woke up, wide-eyed with terror. He gathered his blanket up around him.

"Gregorio, they're here!" Ana cried. "The fight has begun!"

It was still dark outside, but it seemed like a lightning storm was in full force. Bright flashes of light lit the courtyard and doorway in a strange, red glow. Piercing shouts filled the night. Enrique saw men running everywhere in a panic.

Rifles and muskets spat and popped. Cannons fired one after another. Dust and gravel flew as cannon balls slammed into the walls of the courtyard and church.

Enrique realized that it was not even dawn, yet his father grabbed his gun and kissed his wife goodbye. Gregorio paused at the door. He looked back fondly at his children, then he dashed out into the battle.

SLAM!

BOOM!

The men outside barked warnings at each other. "They're coming over the walls!"

Suddenly, a man appeared in the doorway, breathing heavily from running. "Whatever you do, Ma'am, stay in here!" he shouted, and then he was gone.

CRASH!

The walls of the little room shook, throwing dust on everyone. Enrique's brothers screamed, and the baby cried.

"Fall back, fall back!" someone yelled.

There was a steady thunder of gunfire as the battle raged, worse this time than it had ever been since they arrived at the Alamo. The courtyard was bathed in the red light of fire and explosions.

BOOM! The ground shook and rumbled with the fury of the fight.

After what seemed like an eternity, the sun began to come up outside. Ana covered her children with a blanket, and Enrique covered his ears with his hands, trying to shut out the deafening noise of the battle. He had no idea how long it lasted.

All at once a soldier burst inside his family's room! Enrique peeked out from under the blanket, only to see that the soldier was pointing a gun at them!

Just then, another of Santa Anna's soldiers stormed into the room. He was dressed in a nicer uniform than the first soldier, which meant that he was an officer of higher rank. The officer glanced at Enrique and his family, then pushed the other soldier out of the way.

"Stop!" the officer shouted at the soldier. "Families are not to be harmed. Get out of here!"

The soldier lowered his gun and backed out through the doorway.

"Madam, come with me to safety," the officer said to Ana. "You and your children will not be harmed."

Leaving everything behind, the officer led them out into the courtyard.

The sun was all the way up now, and in the daylight, the Alamo was a very different place. Santa Anna's soldiers were everywhere, marching in lines, running here and there, firing their guns into open doorways and windows. Cannons still fired from time to time, but much less often now.

Enrique's family was joined by other families

led by other officers, and together they were all marched out the main gate of the Alamo and down the street to the house of Señor Musquiz, Enrique's neighbor. When they all arrived inside, however, they found the house full of soldiers who were using it as a place from which to run their army.

"Stay here," commanded the officer.

Enrique was confused. He could barely recognize this as his neighbor's house. He knew that he was still in San Antonio, but everything seemed so different!

The yard where he used to play with his friends, his school, the garden he'd helped his mother build—there was now only a world of fighting, guns, and strange soldiers.

And he had not seen his father since that morning.

After an hour or more, another officer came into the Musquiz house. He went up to Ana and said, "You and your family are to be brought before His Excellency."

Enrique could not believe his ears. Did that mean Santa Anna?

Ana gathered her children close to her, then the officer took them down the street to another house. This house was also full of soldiers, and in the main room stood a wide table. A man sat at the table, wearing the fanciest, most decorated uniform Enrique had ever seen. It sent a chill through his entire body.

The man sitting before them was the one Enrique had seen in the town square when the soldiers first arrived in San Antonio. This was the man everyone feared—Santa Anna, ruler of all Mexico.

"Come forward," Santa Anna commanded. His voice echoed all around the room.

Ana held her children close to her. She stood straight and tall as they walked slowly toward the table. Enrique saw that his mother looked Santa Anna right in the eye and did not blink.

"Woman, where is your husband?" asked Santa Anna.

Ana swallowed hard, her jaw tight, and said simply, "He is in the Alamo." She did not call Santa Anna *Sir* or *Excellency* as the soldiers had.

"Do you have any other family?" he asked.

"Yes," Ana said. "My husband's brother, Francisco, is a soldier in your army."

The leader of the Mexican army looked at Ana for a long time, then moved his gaze to the children. When his eyes met Enrique's, Enrique thought his legs might give out beneath him. But he thought of his brave mother, swallowed hard, and looked the man straight in the eye.

Santa Anna studied them for what seemed like ages. When he finally did speak, he said, "You are free to go."

He motioned to an officer, who stepped forward. The officer held out a folded blanket in one hand and two *pesos* in the other. Ana stared at him as though she were angry with him, and Enrique couldn't at first understand why.

After a long moment, she took the items and turned to her family. "Let's go home," was all she said.

As they left the house, Enrique saw black columns of smoke rising into the sky from the direction of the Alamo. He began to slowly realize that the Alamo had been lost and his father was probably gone forever. That was why his mother had stared at the officer like she had. Her husband had given his life, and she had been given nothing but blankets and a little money.

Enrique felt safe holding his mother's hand. And as they walked home, he began to feel very proud of his mother and father. He knew that he would live his life doing his best to be just as strong and sure as them.

✥ Epilogue ✥

Enrique Esparza's father, Gregorio, died with the other defenders of the Alamo. Gregorio's brother, Francisco, gained permission from Santa Anna to bury his brother. Eventually, most of the families that had fled San Antonio returned, reuniting with friends and neighbors.

In 1836, Tejas won its independence from Mexico. It became the Republic of Tejas and was an independent country for nine years. Texas became part of the United States in 1845.

The Esparzas and other families of the Alamo believed in freedom and fought to defend those beliefs. They stood up to those that bullied them, they stood by each other to the end, and their memories stand tall even today.